Be the Best
BMX RACING

A Step-By-Step Guide
By Rod Alexander

Troll Associates

Library of Congress Cataloging-in-Publication Data

Alexander, Rod.
    BMX racing: a step-by-step guide / by Rod Alexander.
        p.   cm.—(Be the best!)
    Summary: Discusses the equipment, techniques, and procedures
associated with BMX racing.
    ISBN 0-8167-1943-8 (lib. bdg.)   ISBN 0-8167-1944-6 (pbk.)
    1. Bicycle motocross—Juvenile literature.   [1. Bicycle
motocross.   2. Bicycle racing.]   I. Title.   II. Series.
GV1049.3.A44   1990
796.6'2—dc20   89-27291

Be the Best
BMX RACING

A Step-By-Step Guide

FOREWORD

by Art Barda

BMX racers dip, zip, turn, churn, and soar around the track toward the finish line. What BMX racers put into a competition is what they get out of it. They're on their own out there. And that makes the sport very exciting to be in and also to watch.

Winning at BMX racing takes dedication, concentration, and physical fitness. It's a sport full of fun, and it's a great way to meet new friends. BMX racing also builds self-confidence and provides a deep feeling of accomplishment.

What I like about this book is that it explains the basics of BMX racing clearly and simply.

Art Barda

Art Barda is a nationally known expert in both BMX racing and motorcycle racing. For four years, he owned a major BMX racing team. For fifteen years, he was a nationally ranked dirt-track motorcycle racer. And he has set four speed records at the Bonneville Salt Flats in Utah. Art is currently the professional dirt-track manager for the American Motorcyclist Association.

Contents

What Is BMX Racing?

BMX, or bicycle motocross, racing is an exciting, competitive sport rapidly growing in popularity among young athletes everywhere. What makes BMX racing so appealing to youngsters is that it is designed specifically for them. Most bicycle motocross races are open only to boy and girl riders aged five to nineteen.

However, BMX racing is anything but a childish sport. Races are fast-paced, thrilling, and even a little dangerous. Sometimes there are spills, falls, and minor collisions. Serious injuries are very rare because of the sport's safety rules and special protective equipment. But there is always a possibility of getting bumps, bruises, scratches, and scrapes. That is why it takes something special to be a BMX racer. You need courage, stamina, strength, and balance. But most of all, you need physical and mental toughness. You also need proper equipment.

If you think you might like pedaling a bicycle around hairpin turns and curves and over bumps, jumps, and other obstacles, then BMX racing is a sport you'll probably enjoy.

BMX RACER

BMX Racing—
Then and Now

The word *motocross* is a combination of two other words: *motorcycle* and *cross-country*. And that's what a motocross is: a race in which motorcycles are ridden cross-country style over a course laid out with obstacles on rugged terrain. Bicycle motocross, or BMX, is a motocross meant for bicycles only.

Compared to most other sports, BMX racing is fairly new. It probably started around 1969 in California. But BMX racing has its roots in motocross racing that became formally organized in Europe in 1952. Lightweight motorcycles specially built for off-road racing were used then as they are now. They'd race around a looping course complete with jumps, bumps, water hazards, and sand and mud obstacles.

MOTOCROSS MOTORCYCLE

Many California boys and girls were big fans of motocross racing. They enjoyed watching it on TV. But most of them were not old enough to ride motorcycles. So they began racing their bicycles in motocross fashion around 1969.

Ordinary street bikes, however, had trouble standing up to the bumps and jumps of motocross racing. They often bent, broke, or fell apart. That's when young BMX racers started modifying their bikes with special equipment. These modifications made the bikes more adaptable to off-road and dirt-track racing. Those early modified bikes, along with the small Sting-Ray bikes intro-

**SCHWINN 'STING-RAY' BIKE
THE FIRST BMX BIKE**

duced by the Schwinn Bicycle Company in the early 1970s, gave birth to the modern BMX-style bike.

BMX racing fever quickly spread all over California in the 1970s. Youngsters were racing on back yard tracks and in open fields everywhere.

Motorbike motocross promoters were quick to recognize a good thing when they saw it. Many scheduled bicycle motocross races before their regular motorbike motocross races. That brought the sport of BMX racing out of vacant lots and into the limelight.

In 1973, the first formal BMX clubs and associations were formed to govern and regulate the new sport. Shortly afterward, BMX racers moved off of motorcycle motocross tracks and onto shorter tracks designed exclusively for bicycle motocross. Specialized BMX bikes also appeared for sale in bike shops around the country. BMX racing had finally arrived.

Amazingly, the bike sport that began in the back yards, lots, and fields of California quickly spread. Today, BMX races are held at local, regional, and national levels by a variety of sponsoring organizations. At the local and regional levels, they can include Police Athletic Leagues, Boys Clubs of America, and YMCAs.

At the national level, the two largest BMX organizations you can join are the National Bicycle League (NBL), founded in 1976, and the American Bicycle Association (ABA), founded in 1977. Both the NBL and the ABA oversee and approve races across the country. And from specified races emerge BMX champions in different classifications (see page 37).

At the international level, BMX races and individual pro riders can be sponsored by companies (often bike manufacturers). These pro riders tour the world, competing for cash prizes. Pro riders must be at least fourteen years old, and they are all among the best riders in the sport today.

Yes, BMX racing is one of the youngest sports around. But it is growing every year.

A FAMILY AFFAIR

You can learn to be a BMX rider on your own, but the sport of BMX racing is usually a family project. Racing is not something you can do completely by yourself. Today, there is a certain amount of expense involved for the special bike and equipment needed to race. But don't be alarmed. It's not that costly. Secondhand bikes and gear are often available, and riders sometimes share or borrow equipment such as helmets.

In addition, parents and relatives are needed to bring young racers to the tracks to compete. A parent or guardian must sign a special permission slip before you will be allowed to race. You can't just show up on your own with a bike and hope to compete.

But BMX racing isn't a chore. It's a fun way for a family to spend time together. There are many ways to get involved in a BMX race. And just being a spectator is fun enough by itself.

Safety Gear

BMX tracks are designed to be difficult and demanding, but *not* dangerous. Yet racers still fall or bump into other racers. And that's why BMX racing requires special safety gear. It helps prevent any serious injuries, which are rare in the sport anyway.

If you want to, you can spend a lot of money on BMX gear. Wearing a flashy outfit can be part of the fun of BMX racing. But keep in mind that the best-dressed racer is not necessarily the best rider in a BMX race. *Always* dress for safety first. Besides, how sharp you look has nothing to do with how well you compete.

The safety gear that follows is required on all BMX tracks.

13

HELMETS AND FACE PROTECTION

The helmet is the most important piece of equipment for a BMX racer. *Never* buy a cheap helmet that could crack or split because you want to save a little money. Buy the best helmet you can get. It will protect you better and keep you safe.

There are two basic types of helmets worn by BMX racers. The first one is called a *full-face helmet*. This helmet fits completely over the head and protects the jaw and chin as well as the head. It will give you the best face protection.

FULL-FACE HELMET

Sun
Visor

Goggles

Some riders complain that the full-face helmet is a bit heavy and uncomfortable. Others feel it limits their vision to just the track straight ahead. But there are other BMX racers who feel that the track straight ahead is all they need to see.

The second type of helmet worn by BMX racers is an *open-face helmet*. It covers the entire head, but is open in the front so a rider's entire face is visible. This helmet allows you to see riders behind and to the sides of you. But there is no protection for the jaw, chin, or mouth.

OPEN-FACE HELMET

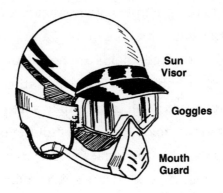

Sun Visor

Goggles

Mouth Guard

That's why many riders who wear the open-face helmet also wear a cuplike plastic guard that attaches to the helmet with straps and protects the chin, jaw, and mouth. For even more protection, many BMX racers wearing open-face helmets will use a separate plastic mouth guard.

Which of the two helmets is better? There is no answer to that question. They are both good helmets. You will have to decide which one is best for you.

When picking a helmet, make sure it fits snugly but not too tightly. The padding inside should be spongy and comfortable but not too soft. Soft padding can compress too quickly if the helmet is hit hard. And that can result in injury. Firmer padding helps absorb shock better.

Some racers like to attach sun visors to their helmets. Visors are not required by BMX safety rules, but they do help to keep sun and grit out of your eyes. Another way to keep sun and track dust out of your eyes is to wear safety goggles with elastic straps that fit over your helmet.

Some BMX racers prefer to attach face shields instead of goggles to their helmets. Face shields are made of clear plastic. They snap onto the helmet and protect the entire face. Like visors, face shields are not required safety gear.

But whether you wear visors, face shields, goggles, or some combination of all three, make sure they're shatter-proof. The same holds true for regular eyeglasses. If you wear them, be sure the lenses won't break into pieces if struck. It's also a good idea to wear a face shield if you wear eyeglasses while racing. Again, safety should be uppermost in your mind.

Face Shield

A good helmet can usually last three or more years. But it is a good idea to play it safe and get a new helmet about every two or three years.

Check your helmet after each race for cracks, dents, or other signs of wear and tear. A helmet with even the smallest crack should be replaced.

You should also regularly inspect the padding inside your helmet. If the padding becomes too hard or too compressed, or if it's torn or split, have it replaced at a sporting goods store. This may seem like a lot of work and worry over a helmet. But remember, you can never be too safe. The body you're protecting is your own.

CLOTHING

Wearing the proper clothing is important if you want to escape without too many scratches and scrapes. BMX tracks will not allow racers to compete without proper safety clothing.

Pants Regulations require that all riders wear long pants. The best BMX pants are made of heavy-duty nylon fabrics with padded knees covered by leather. The seat, hip, and shin areas are also padded. Pants and jerseys are available in matching sets and come in many bright colors.

If you cannot afford BMX pants, you can get by with heavy, straight-cut jeans that do not hang below your ankles and are not too bulky at the ankles. If you do wear jeans, kneepads are a must.

REGULAR CLOTHES

Old Shirt

Borrowed Helmet

Elbow Pads

Jeans

Kneepads

High-Top Sneakers

Jerseys The jersey, or shirt, worn by a BMX rider should have long sleeves. Some tracks allow riders to race with short sleeves if they wear elbow pads. Regulations require either long sleeves or elbow pads. Wear both if you can.

The best BMX shirt you can wear is made of nylon and has padding already sewn into the elbow areas. It resembles a football jersey.

TYPICAL BMX RACING OUTFIT

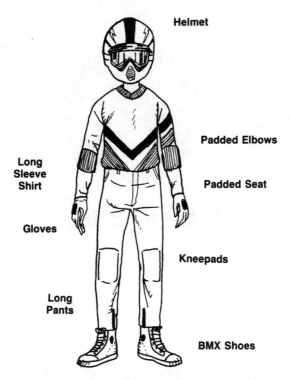

Helmet

Padded Elbows

Long
Sleeve
Shirt

Padded Seat

Gloves

Kneepads

Long
Pants

BMX Shoes

Shoes BMX shoes are special sneakers with padded tongues and collars. They are made of heavy-duty nylon and have soles that provide good traction. But they are expensive, so you may have to wear regular sneakers instead. If you do, make sure they're high-top sneakers with soles that are not too smooth.

Gloves Although not required, gloves are worn by most BMX racers. They prevent blisters from forming on your hands while you grip your bike's handlebars. And they help protect your hands during slide-out or slow-speed spills on the track. All-leather or leather-and-nylon racing gloves are best for BMX riding.

BMX Bike

A BMX bike has to take a lot of physical punishment. It must also meet certain safety regulations. That makes the BMX bike special.

Bikes used for BMX racing have no fenders, chain guards, or reflectors. They are smaller and more compact than regular street bikes. BMX bikes have customized parts such as special tires, handlebars, and lightweight seats. Their frames are specially designed to withstand the pressures of off-road racing. That is why there is usually little difference between girls' and boys' BMX bikes. Both types have a top tube bar across the middle for extra support and strength. In addition, regulation BMX bikes must have padding across the handlebars, gooseneck (see page 24), and top tube.

Using customized parts, you can assemble your own BMX bike. Or you can buy a factory-assembled one from a bicycle shop.

STREET BIKE

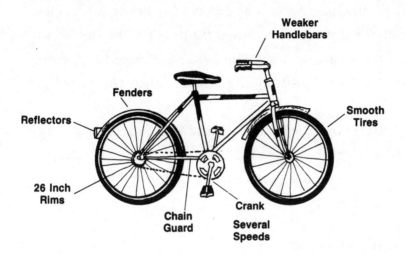

Weaker Handlebars

Fenders

Reflectors

Smooth Tires

26 Inch Rims

Chain Guard

Crank

Several Speeds

BMX BIKE

Stronger Handlebars For Extra Support

Light-Weight Seat

Pads

No Reflectors

No Fenders

Thick Fork

20 Inch Rims

Crank

One Speed

BMX FRAME

A BMX frame is basically metal tubing welded in a special way to hold the individual parts together under the great stress of BMX racing. The frame has a top tube, which must be padded, and a down tube. This is what is known as a *closed frame.* (It's like the frame in a boys' street bike.) The best BMX bike frames are constructed of a strong, light steel called *chrome-alloy* or *chrome-moly.*

Even though the basic BMX frame is extremely sturdy, it is lighter than most bike frames. Usually, it weighs under five pounds. A light frame helps you move faster and maneuver more quickly.

BMX BIKE FRAME

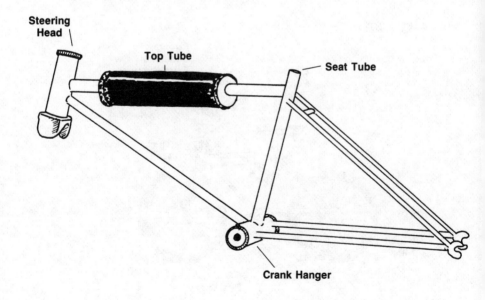

Steering Head

Top Tube

Seat Tube

Crank Hanger

FORK

The fork is found at the front part of the bike. (It looks like a two-pronged fork held downward.) The front wheel and the handlebars are connected to it. The fork is inserted into the bottom of the steering head, or head tube, of the frame. To withstand jumps, bumps, and spills better, BMX forks are much thicker than the forks found on street bikes.

BMX FORK

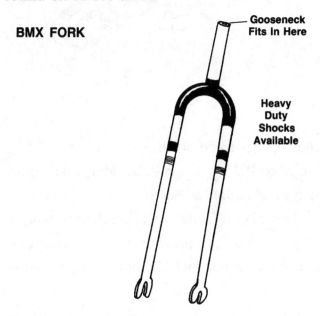

Gooseneck
Fits In Here

Heavy
Duty
Shocks
Available

CRANK

The crank is the piece of metal that connects the pedal to the sprocket wheel. The crank turns the sprocket wheel, which revolves the chain. That, in turn, makes the back wheel spin. On BMX bikes, the cranks are longer and stronger than on regular bikes. The BMX rider can pedal hard with these cranks, which provide extra power and leverage.

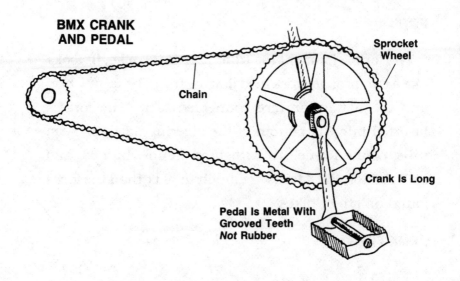

BMX CRANK AND PEDAL

Sprocket Wheel

Chain

Crank Is Long

Pedal Is Metal With Grooved Teeth *Not* Rubber

PEDALS

The regular, rubber-tread pedals used on street bikes are seldom used on BMX bikes. A BMX rider's foot could slip off that type of pedal too easily.

BMX racing pedals are usually all metal, with jagged teeth that grip the foot and prevent it from slipping.

Rarely, if ever, will you see a BMX rider using toe clips on the pedals. These metal cages with straps that fit around the front of the shoe are just too awkward to use. BMX riders can't get their feet out of them fast enough on turns or during slides.

HANDLEBARS

The gooseneck is the piece of curved metal that clamps your handlebars to the fork. The handlebars of a BMX bike also have an extra bar, or crossbar, across the

V-section to give it added strength. Regulations require that both the gooseneck and the crossbar on the handlebars be padded.

Hand grips on the ends of handlebars are also required. Bare metal at the handlebar ends is not allowed to show. Avoid hard-plastic and odd-shaped grips. They can give you blisters and are more likely to slip off during a race. Round, soft-rubber grips with a good tread pattern on them are probably the best ones to use. But no matter what grips you use, gloves are recommended for BMX racing.

A numbered identification plate is required on every bike entered in a bicycle motocross. The plate is slung between and attached to the handlebars.

BMX HANDLEBARS

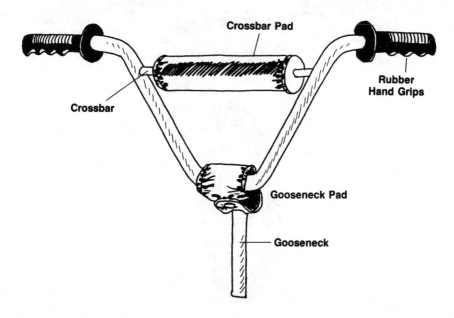

Crossbar Pad

Rubber
Hand Grips

Crossbar

Gooseneck Pad

Gooseneck

WHEELS, BRAKES, AND TIRES

Most BMX bikes have wheels twenty inches in diameter. That is the standard racing size.

BMX bikes used for racing, not riding, are *freewheel* bikes. That means you can only pedal these bikes forward. You can't backpedal to brake. That's why freewheel bikes require *caliper brakes*, the kind usually found on ten-speed street bikes.

Caliper brakes are small rubber pads attached to the front and rear rims of your wheels. A small lever mounted on your handlebars operates them. The lever and brakes are connected by cable. Squeeze the lever, and the caliper brakes press against the rims, slowing and stopping the bike.

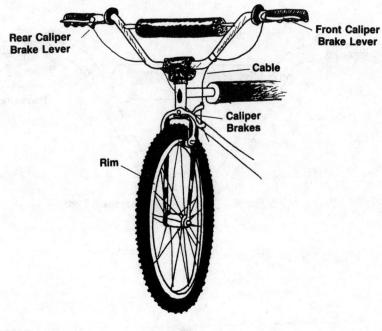

Rear Caliper
Brake Lever

Front Caliper
Brake Lever

Cable

Caliper
Brakes

Rim

BMX bikes used for riding, not racing, have *coaster brakes.* Common to most street bikes, coaster brakes mean you reverse the pedal and brake. The reason why coaster brakes are not good for BMX racing is that racers often have to stand on their pedals for balance and to take jumps. And with coaster brakes, they might stop their bikes on the track without wanting to. Coaster brakes are much better for freestyle, or stunt, riding on BMX bikes.

**FREESTYLE RIDING
BMX RIM**

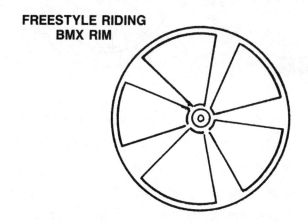

The wheels on BMX racing bikes usually have strong but thin metal spokes. Sometimes, BMX racers put a light, hard-plastic cover over them. That's to protect the spokes from breaking if another racer's pedal hits them by accident. But most BMX racers use spoked wheels without covers. Any extra weight, no matter how light, can slow a racer down.

Freestyle (stunt or trick) riding is generally harder on a BMX bike than racing is. That's why the spokes in freestyle BMX wheels are thicker and stronger. These wheels usually have five thick metal spokes each. They're made to take the punishment of stunt riding.

Smooth   Knobby

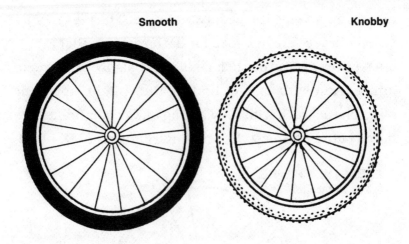

BMX tires differ greatly from smooth street tires. For BMX racing, you need *knobby* tires. Knobby tires have rubber lugs molded into the tread. The lugs dig into the earth on dirt tracks and really speed you along. Knobby tires also grip better on turns and on bumpy surfaces. However, knobby tires are not good for riding on streets or hard-packed surfaces.

BMX Track

BMX tracks have come a long way from the vacant lot courses and motorcycle motocross tracks used for racing in the 1970s. Today, there are commercially run tracks that are exclusively for BMX races. And a number of BMX tracks built on public lands are sponsored by civic and youth organizations.

No two BMX tracks are exactly alike. The land available for the track determines how the track will be laid out. Some BMX tracks have longer straight-aways, wider turns, and more bumps. The variations are almost unlimited. However, to be a real BMX course, each track must have certain things. How those things are arranged is up to each track's designer. From start to finish, a BMX track is usually 800 to 1,400 feet long. And between the start and finish are several turns and various obstacles such as jumps, dips, and bumps.

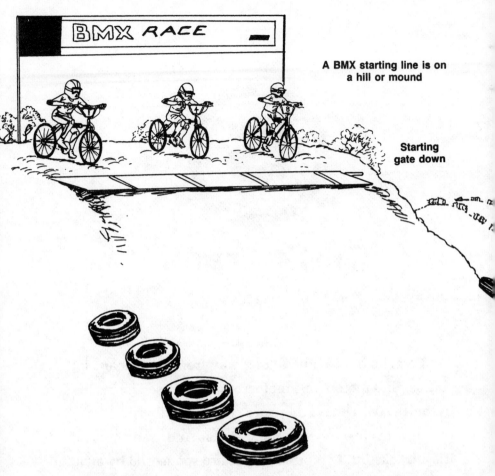

A BMX track's starting line is usually at the top of a small mound, hill, or ramp. Riding down a slope at the beginning gives racers a chance to gain speed quickly at the start of a race.

Most BMX tracks have multiple turns. That increases the difficulty of the course. Some turns are *hairpin* turns, which are U shaped and cause riders to change direction quickly. Other turns are wide sweeping ones with steep banks riders can ride up on. Those high dirt banks are called *berms*. Berms allow riders to take the turn at high speeds.

RIDING CORNERS

Riding the berm

Between the course turns are various obstacles. Sometimes the obstacle is a group of small bumpy mounds called *whoop-de-doos.* They are between three and twelve inches high and are usually grouped three in a row. Whoop-de-doos resemble the speed bumps you sometimes see in parking lots. (See page 55 for how to race over whoop-de-doos.)

Racer riding whoop-de-doos, hay bale barriers on side

Other obstacles on a BMX track are hard-packed dirt mounds larger and longer than whoop-de-doos. These are meant for jumps. They come in different shapes and sizes, and sometimes they can come one right after the other. (See pages 52-55 for how to take these jumps.)

Years ago, many BMX tracks also had mud or sand obstacles. They were carry-overs from motorcycle moto-cross racing. But not many BMX tracks include those obstacles today.

Old Car
Tires Barrier
On Side

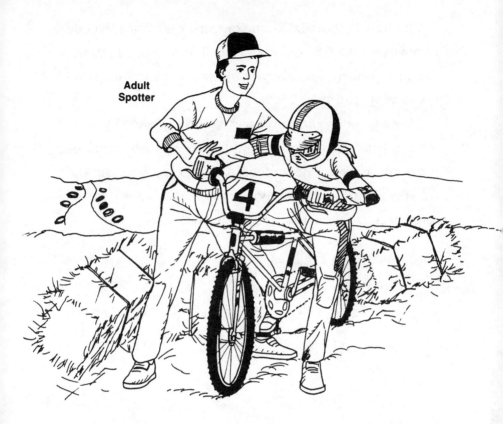

Adult Spotter

The sides of BMX tracks are usually lined with bales of hay, or old car or truck tires. The tires and bales provide a soft landing area should bikers fall. Adult spotters also stand by at appointed areas along the BMX track to assist riders who fall during a race.

INDOOR TRACKS

BMX racing has proved so popular that riders want to race year-round and not be hampered by weather. That's one reason why more and more indoor races have been held in recent years.

The first indoor BMX tracks were very hard, wooden raceways laid out on concrete floors. But they were much *too* hard, and they sometimes made jumps and spills very painful.

These wooden raceways were soon replaced by tracks with actual dirt surfaces, making them seem more like outdoor tracks. The indoor dirt tracks were smaller, however. And even today, indoor BMX tracks are still shorter and faster than outdoor ones.

How a BMX
Race Is Run

Most sports races are run in multiple laps. But there are no laps in BMX racing. Riders go from start to finish only once per race. And each race is called a *moto.*

Usually, six to twelve racers of equal experience compete in a moto. Most BMX races pit the winners of several motos against each other for the championship. Other BMX races award points to the top finishers in each moto. After all the motos are run, the top point getters advance to the final moto. Whoever wins that final moto wins the competition.

Most BMX tracks charge an entry fee for official competitive racing. That means you must pay a certain amount in order to race. Usually, it is only a few dollars.

Many tracks also require a parent or guardian to sign a waiver form. The waiver form states that the track owner or administrators, or race organizers, will not be held legally responsible if you are injured during a race. It is like a permission slip in school. The entry fee you pay usually goes for track maintenance and for professional officials to judge the race.

Before each race, there is an official safety inspection of bicycles and riders' equipment. Any rider or bike that does not meet safety standards (see pages 13-28) will not be allowed to compete.

All BMX riders entered in a race are allowed to take a test run on the track before the actual race is held. A test run helps riders get the feel of the track.

Once the safety inspections and test runs are over, it is time to race.

**BMX HAS A PRE-RACE
SAFETY INSPECTION**

In official BMX races, riders are classified by age and ability. That way, old or experienced riders do not compete against young or inexperienced riders. Some BMX race classifications are:

First-Timer Races   These are for riders who have never competed in BMX before. (For example, if you are ten years old and racing for the first time, you would be entered into the ten first-timer race.)

Beginner Races   These are for riders who have competed before but not yet won a race.

Novice Races   These are for riders who have won at least one BMX race but fewer than five.

Expert Races   These are for riders who have won five or more BMX races.

FIRST-TIMER RACES

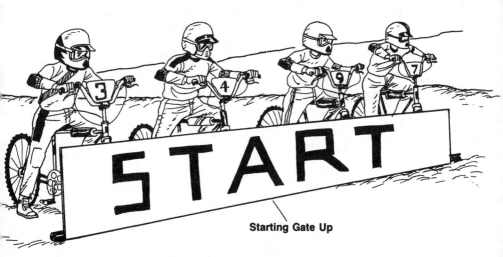

Starting Gate Up

STARTING A RACE

There are several ways to start a race. But as mentioned earlier, the starting line is always on a mound or a hill (see page 30).

A number of BMX tracks today have mechanical starting gates operated by hand. The gate itself is made of wood, metal, or some other material. Riders line up with their bike tires against the gate. The gate blocks their way onto the track.

BMX STARTING GATE

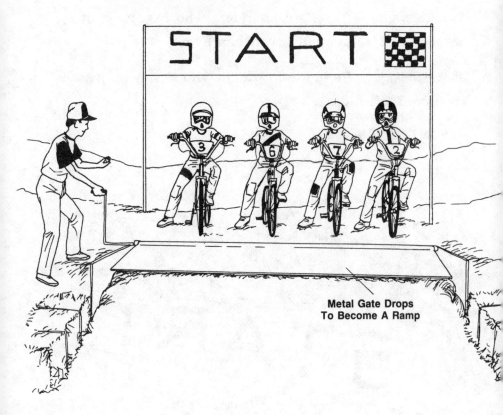

Metal Gate Drops
To Become A Ramp

When the starter sees that all the bikes are in position to race, he or she shouts "Get ready!" That means the race will start momentarily. And when the starter cranks or pushes a lever, the mechanical starting gate falls. The fallen gate then becomes a ramp for racers to get a good downhill start. With a mechanical starting gate, racers really can't anticipate precisely when it will be dropped.

Other tracks have electrically timed starting systems called *Christmas trees*. They got that nickname because they signal the start of the race with flashing red lights. When these lights peak, the starting gate drops automatically and off you go. The lights allow you to anticipate the gate drop, and they make the timing consistent for all starts.

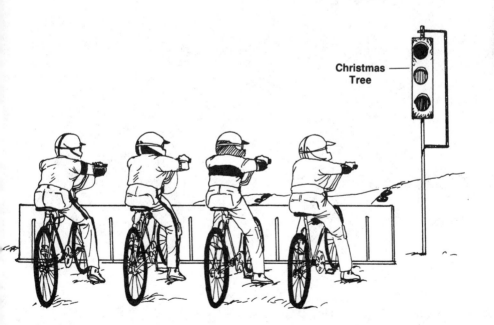

Christmas — Tree

Still another way to begin a BMX race is by a *rubber band start.* In this start, a length of rubberlike tubing is stretched across and suspended above the starting line. Racers line up behind it. When the rubber band drops, the race begins. A rubber band is used because it won't break or snap if riders push against it.

Lastly, a BMX race can be started in the old-fashioned way—with a green flag on a stick. Holding it high in the air, the starter shouts "Riders ready, Pedals ready, Go!" On the word "go," the flag is waved swiftly to the ground, signaling that the race has begun. And at the finish line, the familiar checkered flag is waved as the first rider crosses it.

**RACER GETTING
CHECKERED FLAG
AT FINISH LINE**

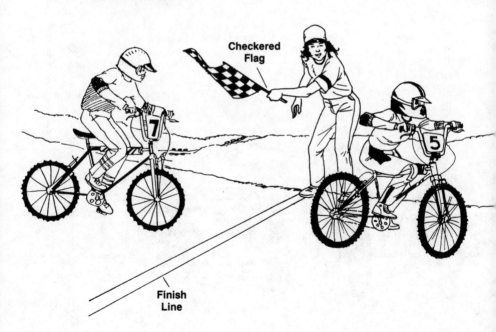

Checkered
Flag

Finish
Line

BMX Riding Techniques

Before you can ride well competitively, you have to learn how to ride efficiently. That means getting the most out of your bike each time you pedal.

BODY POSITION

If you race with your torso straight up on your bike, air pushing against your body will slow you down. That is called *air resistance*. To cut down air resistance, try to ride with your body slightly bent over your bike whenever possible. By keeping slightly hunched over, especially on straight-aways, you will ride much faster.

BODY POSITION ON BIKE

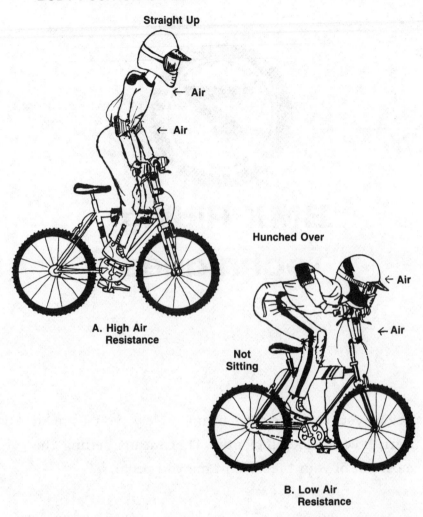

Straight Up

← Air

← Air

A. High Air
Resistance

Hunched Over

← Air

← Air

Not
Sitting

B. Low Air
Resistance

In BMX racing, you have to reach top speed quickly. For the most part, you won't be pedaling sitting down. You will have to learn to maneuver your bike while standing on the pedals. This allows you to get the full force and weight of your body into pedaling. Of course, while standing on the pedals, you are subject to more air resistance. But the tradeoff for more power is worth it.

PEDALING

A. Don't Sit Down

B. Ride Standing In A Hunched-Over Position

PEDALING THE BIKE

When you pedal, try to do it in a smooth, even manner. Don't let your weight shift a great deal with each downward stroke. If you throw all of your weight into each downward stroke, your bike will move in a jerky fashion and your front wheel will wobble slightly. That jerky, wobbly forward motion will make your bike cover more of the track than you have to, and it will slow you down. Remember, the shortest distance between two points is a straight line. The more your front wheel wobbles and veers off course, the farther you have to go.

One way to cut down jerky, uneven pedaling is to keep your knees in close to the bike. That will help keep your legs moving in a straight, up-and-down fashion. Try not to let your knees jut outward as you ride.

KNEE POSITION
FOR PEDALING

Knees out—
wrong way to
.pedal

Right way—
keep knees in close to
bike so they move
straight up and down

Not
heels

Not
toes

Place
balls of feet
squarely on
pedals

Another way to make pedaling more efficient is to position your feet on the pedals correctly. Place the balls of your feet squarely on the pedals. You don't want to pedal with your heels or toes.

BODY-BIKE BALANCE

Keeping proper balance while riding around turns (especially banked turns) is extremely difficult. When making a turn, adjust your body position to the position of the bike as it makes the turn. Think of the bike as part of your body. Lean with the bike as it makes a turn.

Another way to make a turn is to use your leg and foot like a brace. While leaning into a turn, extend the leg on the inside part of the turn. You can even slide the sole of your foot like a balancing ski on the track as you make the turn. In BMX, this is called *hot shoeing*. After hot shoeing, get your foot back on the pedal as quickly as possible.

HOT SHOEING

Use foot as brace by sliding sole on dirt while taking a corner

BMX Racing Techniques

Riding in a real BMX race is a lot different than just riding a street bike. There are certain techniques you should learn.

STARTING

As you know, the start of a BMX race is almost always on a small hill or mound. A good start can give you an advantage over your competition. Remember, the inside of the track is the shortest distance around the track. If you can jump out in front of the pack and snatch the inside position at the start, other racers will have to go around you. Of course, leading at the start of a race doesn't mean you will always finish in the lead. Much can happen during a moto.

There aren't many strict rules you must obey to start a race. You must keep your bike in line and position. And most tracks make you keep one foot on a pedal. Where and how you position that pedal for your first push-off is up to you. You might like the pedal all the way up or halfway down. Experiment with a few different pedal positions to find which one you like best.

PEDAL POSITIONS FOR STARTING

Straight Up   ¾ Way Up   ½ Way Up

You also have to decide which foot you will want to begin pedaling with. Again, experiment to find out if you want to use your right or left foot.

The foot that isn't on a pedal also plays an important part in your start. The foot you place on the ground must shove off to start the bike forward. You have to shove with one foot and start pedaling with the other both at the same time. It is not easy to do, but you will improve in time.

48

BMX STARTING POSITION

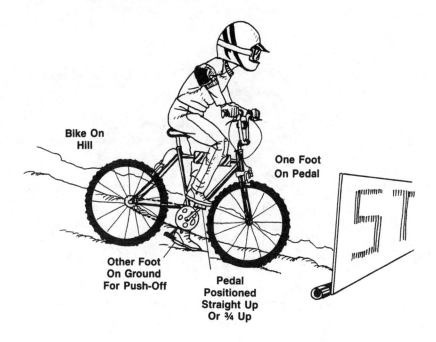

Bike On Hill

One Foot On Pedal

Other Foot On Ground For Push-Off

Pedal Positioned Straight Up Or ¾ Up

Some BMX races do allow a two-pedal start. That means riders have *both* feet on their pedals. They have to balance themselves *and* their bikes against the starting gate. It's not easy, and it takes plenty of practice. But many BMX racers feel a two-pedal start is the best of all.

As you start, keep your front wheel pointed straight down the track. Try not to let your front wheel wobble or weave to the side. Start in a standing crouch position with your seat well back. That shifts weight to the back tire, which will give you more traction. Your torso should lean a bit over the front of the handlebars to prevent you from doing a *wheelie*. A wheelie is when your bike's front tire rises into the air. A wheelie looks great, but it will cost you valuable time at the start of a race.

BIKER DOING WHEELIE

(It looks good but costs you time.)

RIDING CORNERS

Riding corners was discussed a bit in the body-bike balance section (see page 45). One way to take a sharp corner is to hot shoe it (see page 45). During a pre-race test run, you should gauge just how fast you can take every turn on the course.

Sometimes it is better to *ride the berm* on a turn than to hot shoe it in tight. Riding the berm means taking your bike high up the embankment wall. By doing that, you don't drag a foot (hot shoeing), which slows you down. Riding the berm lets you go much faster. However, riding the berm also swings your bike out onto the widest part of the track. And that means you have to ride farther than someone who hot shoes the corner at a sharper angle.

CORNERING

"A" is riding berm

while "B" hot shoes

Knowing how to take a turn is something to experiment with during a test run. It is also a case of which technique you can do better. Cornering is almost always difficult. But it is also one way of passing another bike that may be taking the turn poorly or slowly. Experience is what will make you a good rider in the turns.

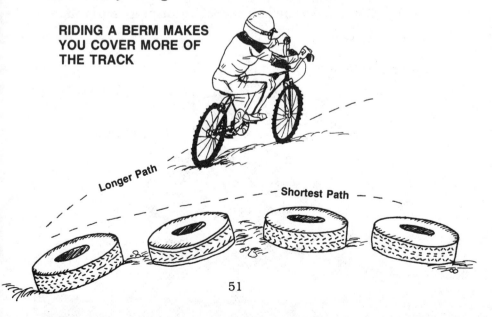

RIDING A BERM MAKES YOU COVER MORE OF THE TRACK

Longer Path

— Shortest Path —

TAKING JUMPS

Taking a bike jump can be a lot of fun. During a race, however, you are not jumping for fun or the applause of onlookers. Your goal is to win the race, and that means taking the jumps the best way possible without losing time.

When you take your test run, go over the jumps slowly and carefully at first. Become very familiar with them. After all, no two jumps are exactly alike. Get a feel for how you should take each one before the race begins.

Also, keep in mind that jumping your bike into the air can be dangerous. Do not try to show off or "hot-dog" over jumps. Always jump the correct way without trying to be flashy.

The correct way to take jumps is to raise your *front* wheel off the ground and to land with your *back* wheel touching down first. What happens if your front wheel touches first? You will most likely go sailing right over the handlebars. So the rule of BMX jumping is to make sure your back wheel hits first.

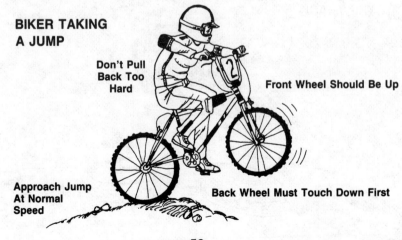

BIKER TAKING A JUMP

Don't Pull Back Too Hard

Front Wheel Should Be Up

Approach Jump At Normal Speed

Back Wheel Must Touch Down First

TAKING A JUMP

1. Do Not Slow Down

2. Keep Weight Back

Lift Handlebars Slightly (Do not jerk or pull them back.)

Let Bike Fly Naturally

3. Do Not Try To Soar Upward Or Hang In Air.

Do Not Pedal

4. Get Weight Forward

Push Down On Handlebars

Back Wheel Touches First

When you are going into a jump, do not slow down. Go into the jump at your regular speed. Try not to jump behind another racer. If he or she crashes, you'll crash right on top of him or her. Try to make sure you have open space ahead for your landing.

When you go up into the air, let your bike fly naturally. Do not try to jump into the air on your bike. Remember, your goal is *not* to set an altitude record. You want to clear the jump as low to the ground as possible.

As you go up, keep your weight back toward your seat while you lift slightly on the handlebars with your hands. That gets the front wheel up so your back wheel will touch down first. Do not pull back on the handlebars too hard or jerk your body backward. That could cause you to do a back flip.

While in the air, most racers keep their bikes straight and do not pedal. They try to keep the pedals parallel rather than up and down. That is an easier position to hold while airborne.

In landing, shift your weight forward the instant your back wheel touches. As you shift your weight, push down on the handlebars to get your front wheel back on the ground. Keep your front wheel pointed straight ahead when it touches down. Once both wheels are back on the track, try to resume top speed as quickly as possible.

RIDING WHOOP-DE-DOOS AND OTHER BUMPS

Whoop-de-doos (see page 31) and other bumps are tough on bikes and riders. During your test run, gauge just how fast you can take these bumps without losing control of your bike. You may not be able to go very fast at first. But with continued practice, you'll increase your speed without losing control of your bike. You want to keep your bike as steady as possible, and you don't want to weave or wobble off to the side.

**RIDING WHOOP-DE-DOOS
IS TOUGH ON THE BIKE
AND THE RIDER**

**Elbows Out Rather
Than Tucked Into Side**

**Try To Hold
Wheel Steady**

One way to help steady the front of your bike is to keep your elbows out from your body rather than in tight near your sides. You also want to keep your weight toward the middle of the bike where the shock of the bumps can be distributed between the two tires. Control of the bike and steadiness are the keys to taking bumps.

Getting the Most Out of Your Bike

A neglected bike can quickly become a faulty bike. So if you want yours to operate at its best all the time, *take care of it.* Right after racing, give your bike a careful, thorough inspection. That way, you can head off any problems, such as a loose seat or a cracked fork, before your next race.

Cleaning your bike should be the next step. Keeping your bike dirt free will cut down wear and tear on such moving parts as chains and wheels.

The rims and wheels should always be checked to make sure they are not bent or misaligned. You can do this by turning your bike upside down. Spin the wheels directly by hand or by turning the pedals to make sure the wheels revolve without wobbling or binding. If they don't spin smoothly, have them repaired and adjusted.

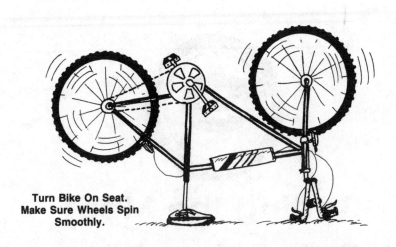

**Turn Bike On Seat.
Make Sure Wheels Spin
Smoothly.**

Another good idea is to make sure the paint on the bike frame isn't chipped or peeling. Paint helps keep metal from rusting. If you have to repaint, make sure there are no cracks in the frame that the new paint will hide. Remember, you're checking to keep yourself safe.

Next, have a parent or a person experienced in bike repairs check your brakes, sprockets, cranks, and chain for problems. It is also a good idea to have an expert remove the chain from your bike and clean it by soaking it in special solvent. Once the chain is cleaned, it can be put back on, correctly tightened (all chains need *some* slack), and lubricated.

Doing all of these things will help keep your bike in top racing condition.

Getting the Most Out of Yourself

Your bike is not the only thing that should be in good condition. *You* should be, too. Stamina and leg strength are what provide the power in BMX racing. So if you want to do well, you'll need both.

The best way to improve your strength and stamina *and* to prepare for BMX racing is to practice over and over again on a track. You can lay out some sort of track in your own back yard, or you can use a nearby field or BMX track. The idea is to race, race, race! The more time you spend pedaling a bike, the better you'll be.

If you do not have room for a track, you can always ride on the street. However, *never* race your BMX bike on paved roads or streets. It is dangerous for you and not good for your bike. You can ride a regular street bike to strengthen your legs and increase your stamina.

SOME WAYS TO GET IN SHAPE

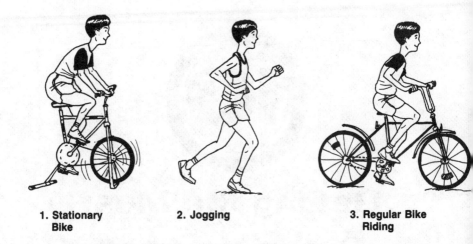

1. Stationary Bike

2. Jogging

3. Regular Bike Riding

Jogging and distance running are two more ways to build up your endurance and leg muscles. Another way is to ride a stationary exercise bike. You can always listen to music, watch TV, or read a book or magazine while exercising on a stationary bike. It doesn't *have* to be boring, and it does work.

Fun for Young
And Old

Usually, BMX racing requires twenty-inch wheels on bikes and is open only to youngsters nineteen or younger. But a remarkable change has occurred in BMX racing during recent years. More and more BMX racers in their twenties and thirties now ride competitively. They enjoy the fun and thrills of BMX racing just as much as younger riders. And one main reason is the development of the BMX *cruiser class.*

BMX cruiser bikes are larger than the standard BMX racing bikes. The very first ones were modified beach cruiser bikes with twenty-six-inch rims. They looked great but were not much good for racing. BMX cruiser bikes have since been reduced to twenty-four-inch

wheels. These have worked out very well, and they are still four inches larger in diameter than the standard racing bike wheels.

But no matter how young or old BMX racers are, they all want to win the races they compete in. In BMX races, especially the large ones, riders are usually given trophies for finishing first in their classifications. In addition, they are awarded No. 1 plates to put on their bikes. This is the goal of every BMX rider who enters a race.

Who knows, with practice and hard work, you may be the next BMX racer to attach a No. 1 plate to your bike. But even if you don't win a race, you can still enjoy BMX racing for all the excitement it provides. So start pedaling and good luck!

INDEX